My horses, I paint them over and over

and over again,

because it's something I cannot do.

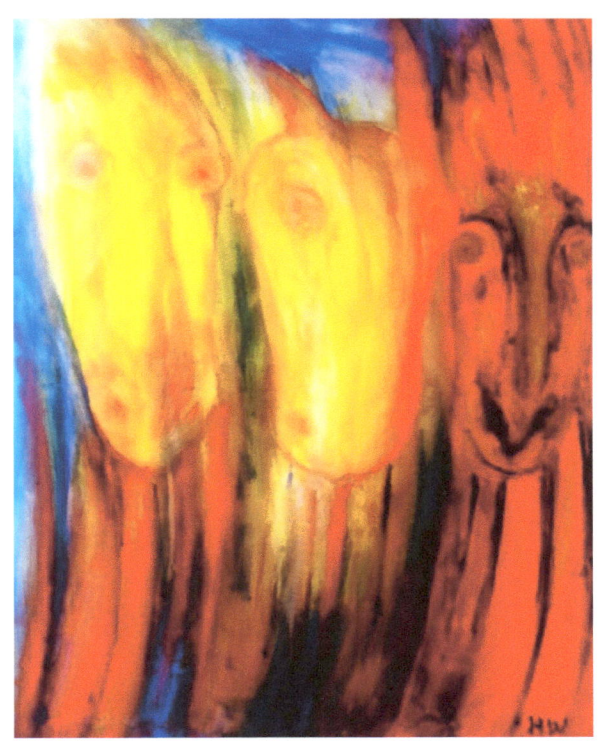

Always the horses

I paint them

All the time

I

have been painting

horses.

It has been

almost

an obsession.

You can see

my mother and

father and me

in the background

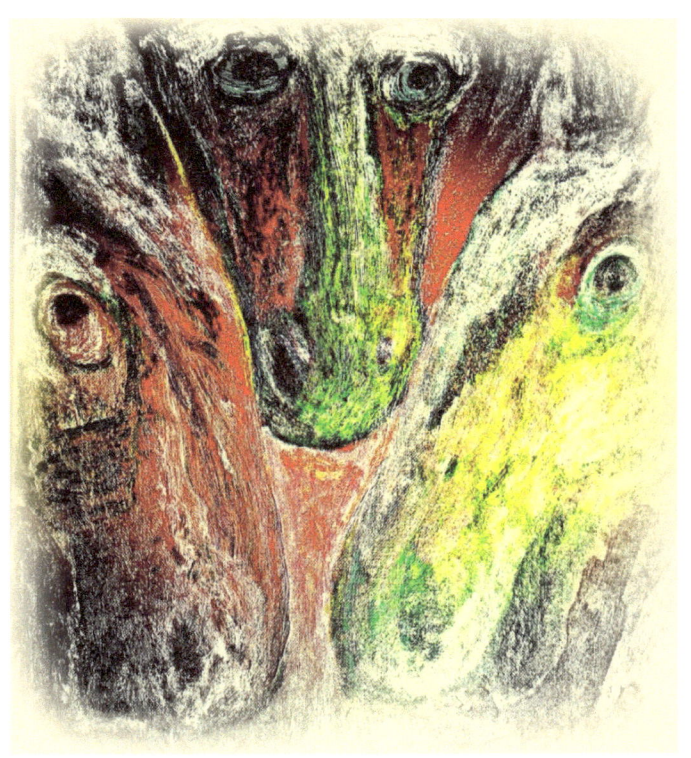

I was born

of a horse

but I was not

a horse.

My horse was

my sister

and I

was her

head and will.

It has been

almost

an obsession.

Some would even

call it

a disaster.

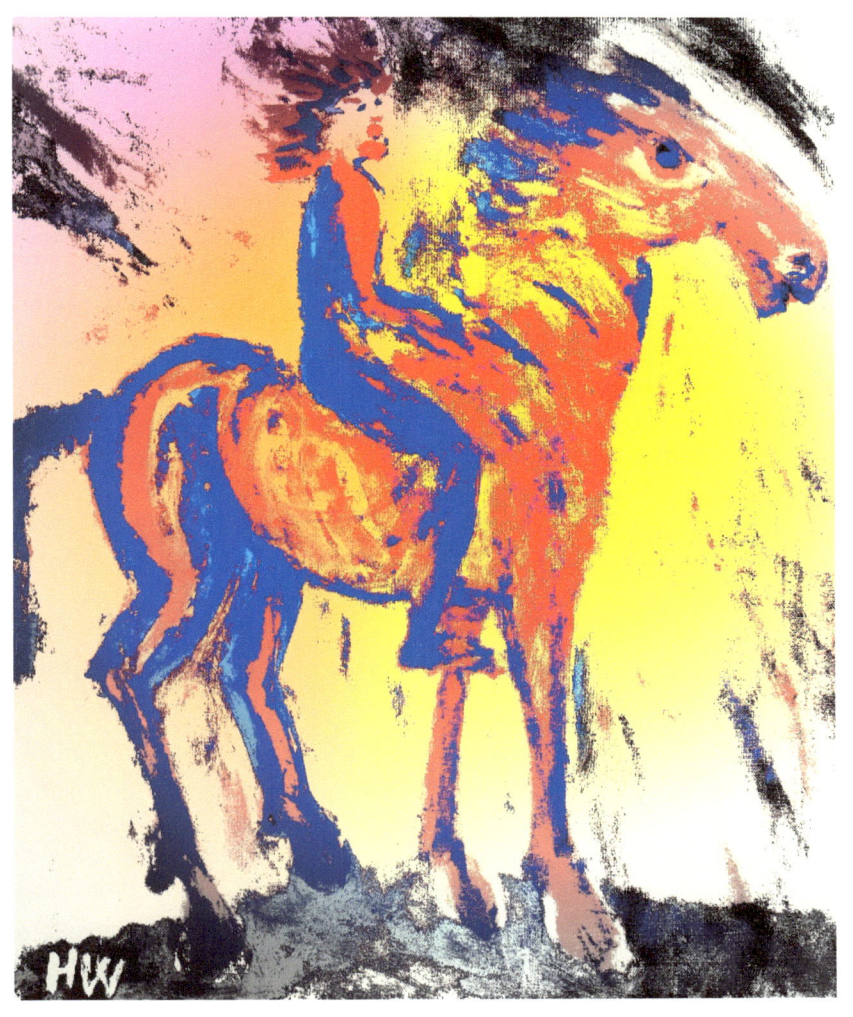

It has been an obsession. For some it might have been a disaster. I wouldn't use such strong words.

I

have always painted

you

my horse.

It has been

almost

an obsession.

Where

did you go?

Why

did she leave me?

My horse,

my

obsession.

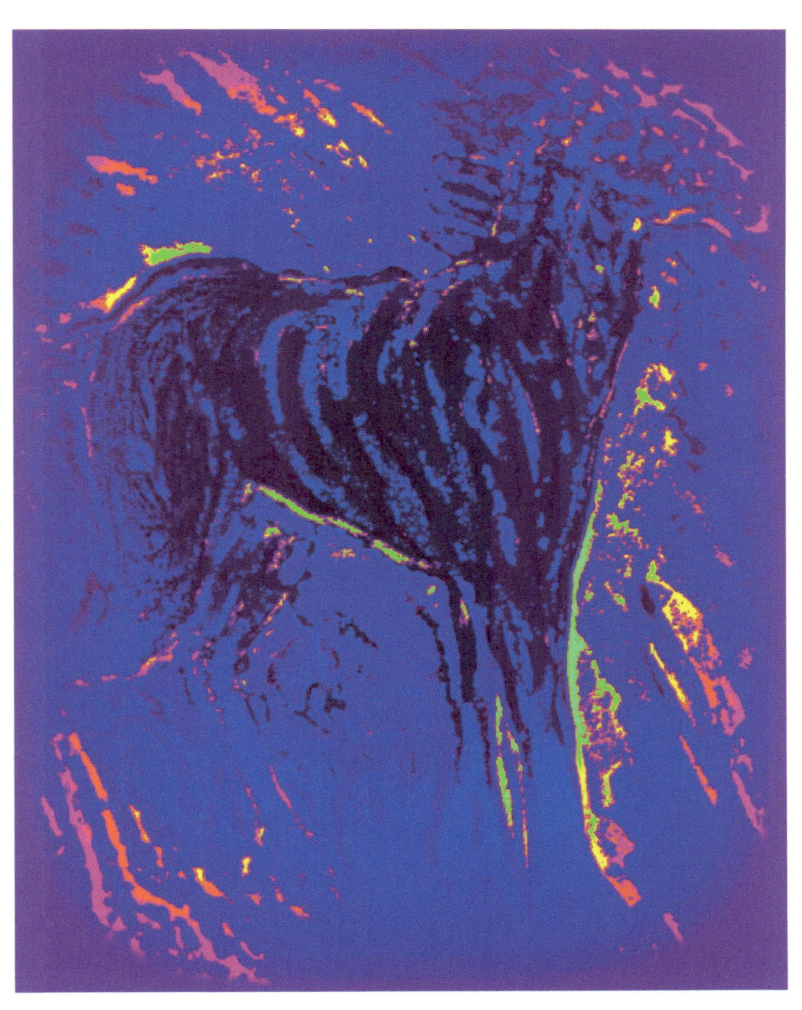

Life

is about love

and loneliness.

Life is about loneliness,
and love is also about life.

You walk, float or spiral
out of reach,
alone
or in your heroic
solitude.

You walk,
float or spiral
out of reach.
I
cannot reach you
anymore.

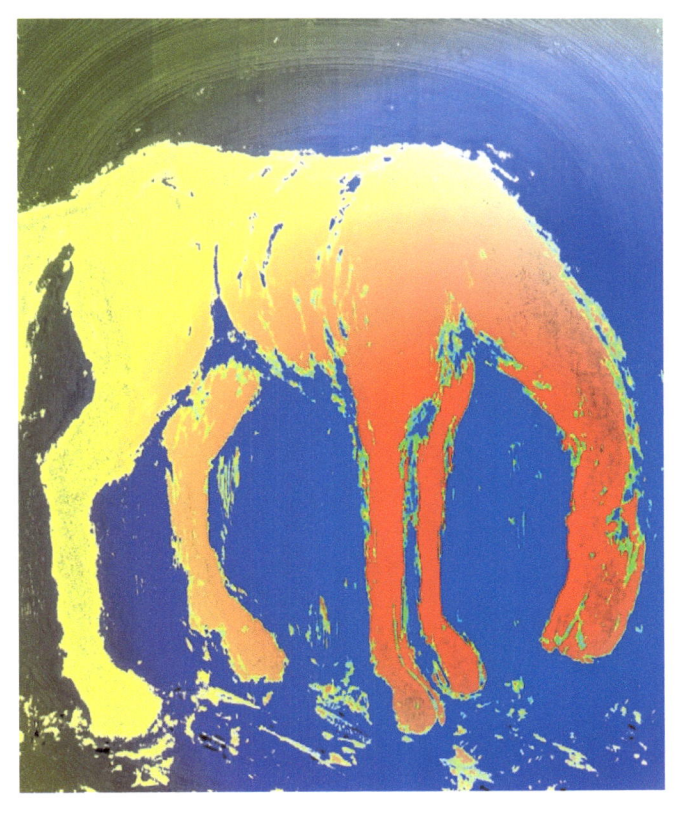

The horse is in me and in you too.

I look forward to the meeting

between me, my painting and my

horse

Life is not

about individuals,

but about timeless

human

existence.

Life is also about

loneliness.

I miss you, my horse.

We were meant to be

Together and never apart or

alone.

You must let go and let the feelings go.

The more insecure and clumsy you are

and the less control you have,

the better will the horse be.

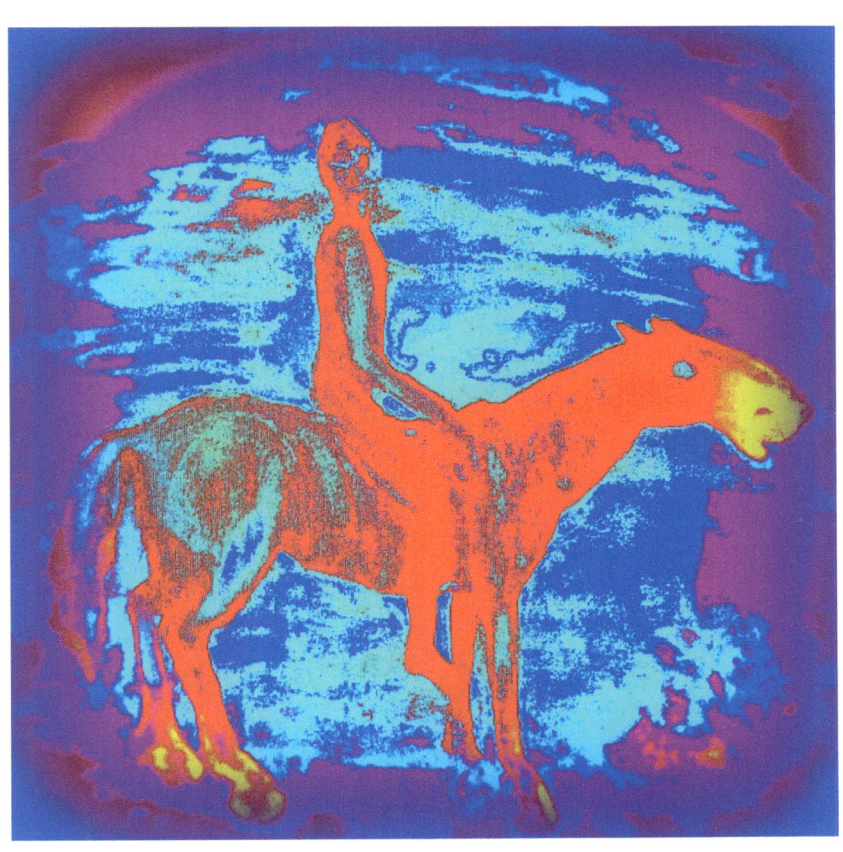

Some

are keen on

control,

to be in control,

to know

what's going on.

Others

devote themselves

to the extent

that they loose

control.

So I go on

painting my horses

because it's something

I cannot do.

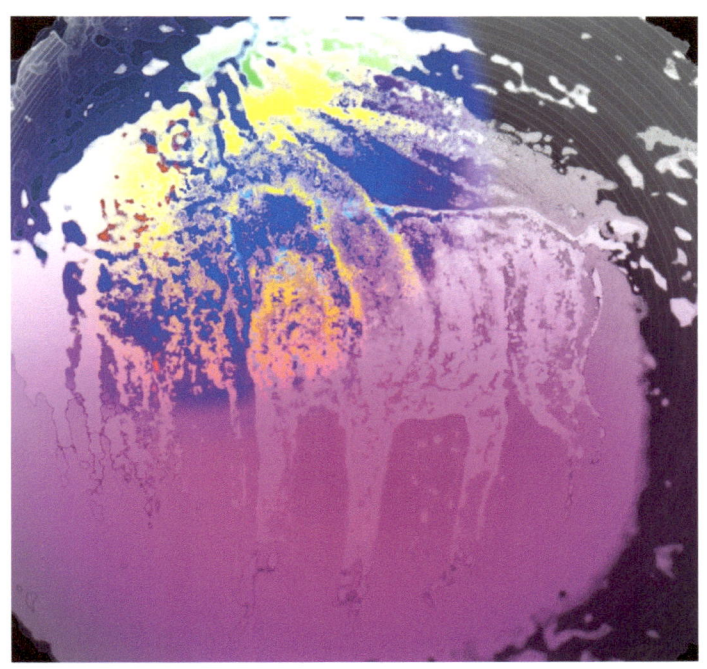

There are swiftly memories

of brushstrokes,

energetic and vibrant.

I have thought a lot
but I'm not good
at listening,
and I'm not good
at discussing
and I do not understand
other people or
their views.
Where
did my horse go?
Why
did she leave me?
I do not understand
other people or
their views.

The horse is in me

and in you too

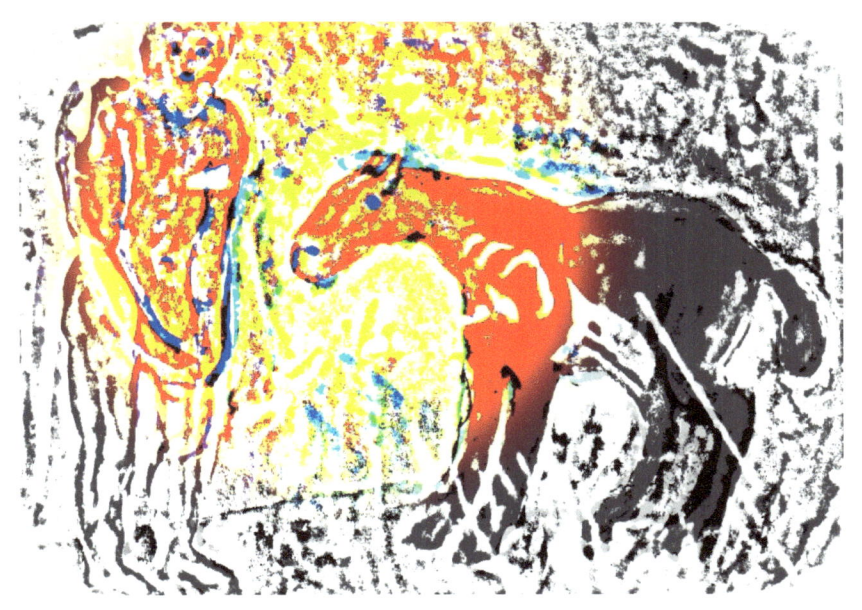

I am looking forward

to a meeting

between me and you

my horse

and the painting.

Black and white horses

can also be colorful.

You have to let go

and let the feelings go.

The more insecure

and clumsy you are

and less control you have,

the better

is the horse

You have to let go

and let the feelings go.

The less control

you have,

the better.

It is not color, but the light I paint.

Look here.

See how the light

illuminates the colors.

The light creates the color.

It is not color, but the light I paint.

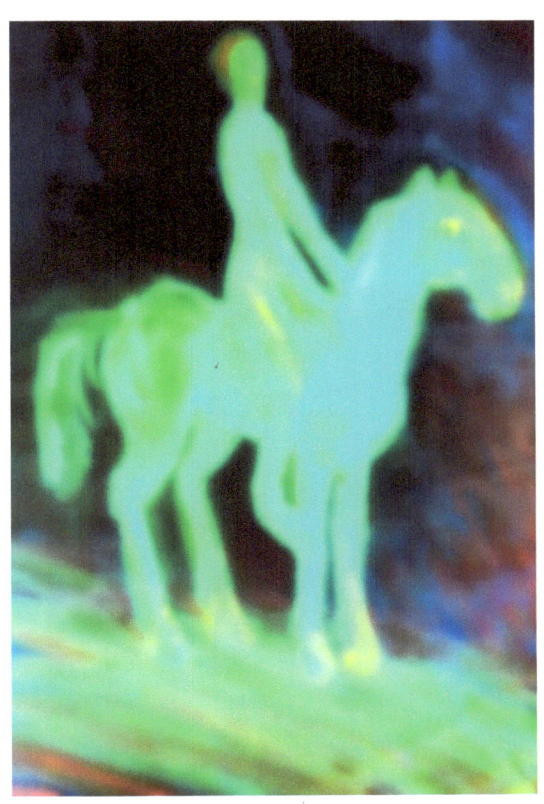

Some are keen

on control,

to be in control,

to know what's going on.

Others

are able to devote

themselves to

the extent

that they lose

control.

They drop out

and hope that

it is soil

where they land.

I have always painted

horses,

it has been almost

an obsession.

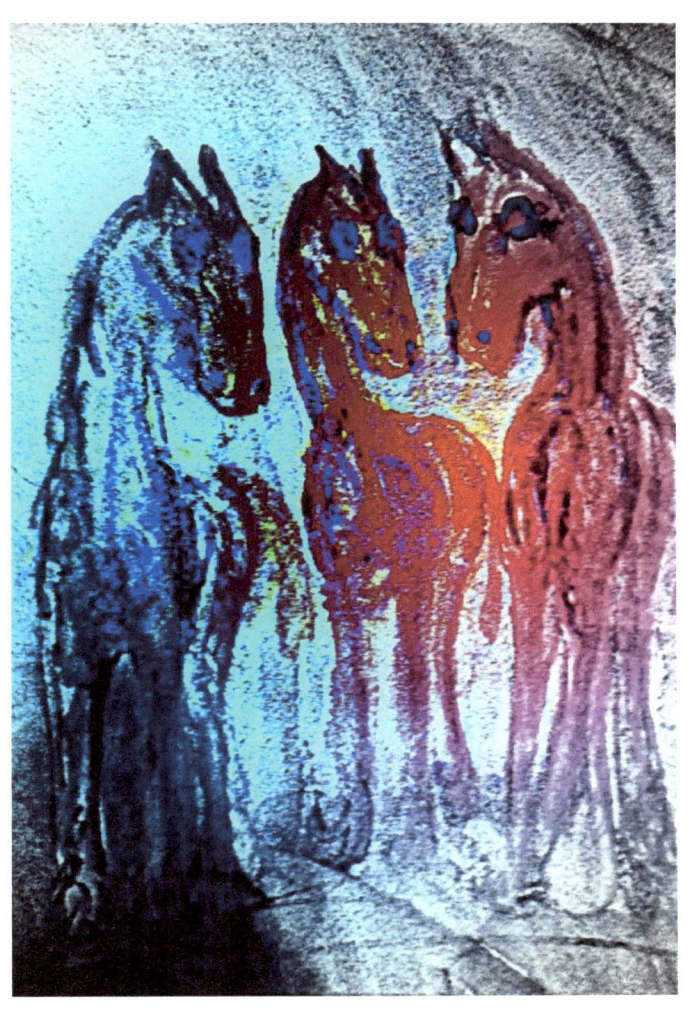

Mother

and father and I

in the background.

I was born of a horse, but

I was not a horse.

My sister was a horse

And I was her head and will.

It has been almost

an obsession.

I have always painted horses.

It has been almost an obsession.

Where did my horse go?

Why did she leave me?

The horse is in me and in you too,

I am looking forward to a meeting

between me, the horse

and the painting.

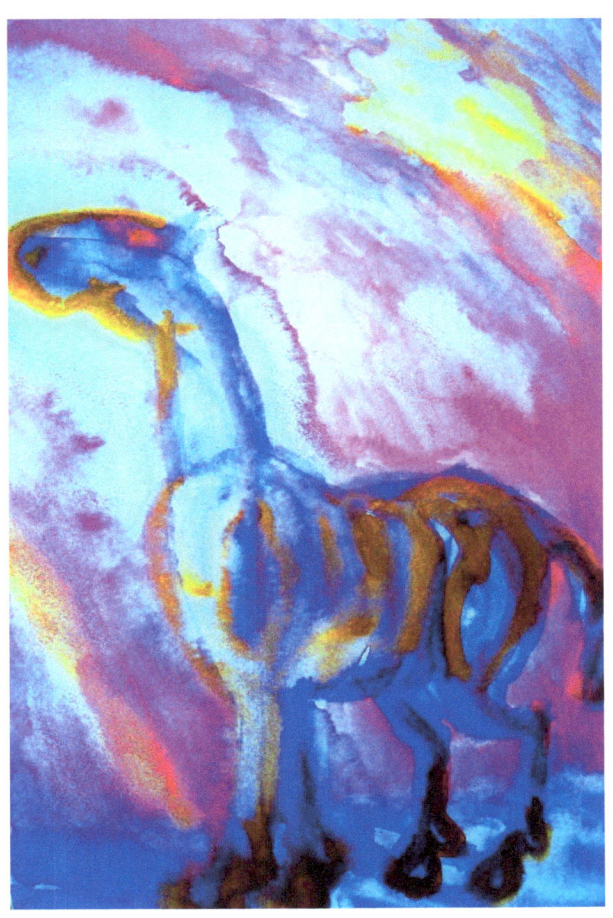

If you are painting
a horse,
you don't know
what it will be
in advance.

You have to let go
and let the feelings go.
The more insecure,
And clumsy you are
and less control you have,
the better is the horse.

Black and white horses

can also be colorful,

just look

at the light

in the woodcut.

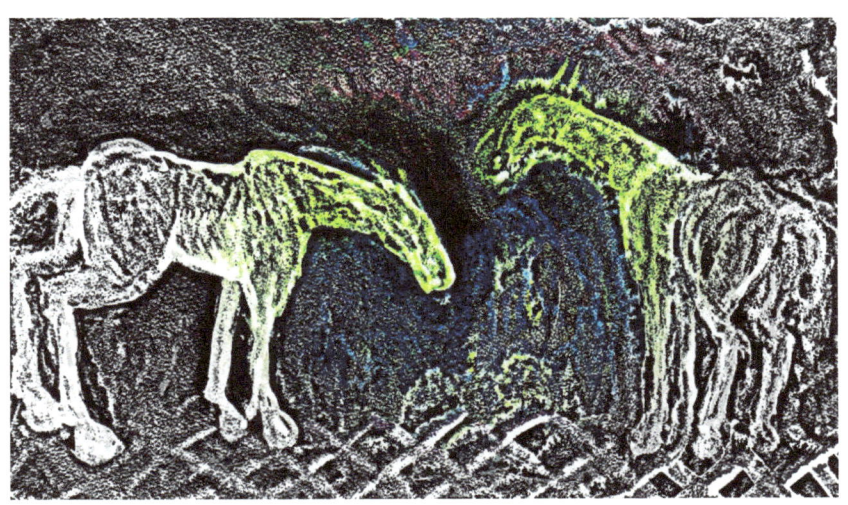

I paint my horses

because it's something

I cannot do.

There are swiftly memories

of the brushstrokes,

energetic and vibrant.

The soul's a horse.

The horse's soul.

Thighs

The feminine.

The sensuous.

A picture of three horses. Mother, father and I in the background. I was born of a horse, but I was not a horse. My sister was a horse, and I was her head and will.

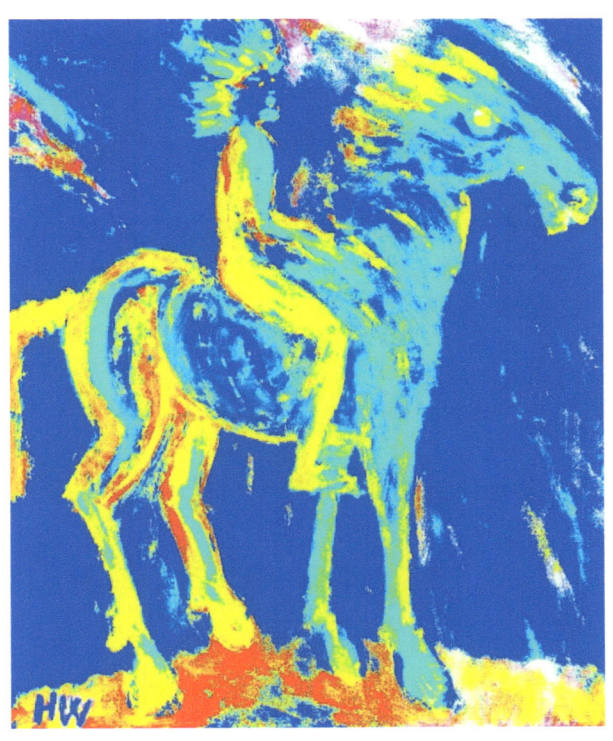

It has been almost

an obsession.

I have always painted

horses.

It has been almost

an obsession.

Where did my horse go.

Why did she leave me.

I have always painted horses.

It has been almost an obsession.

So it's time to fight back

against critics who claim

that I am too superficial.

I was born of a horse,

but I was not a horse.

Where are we now?

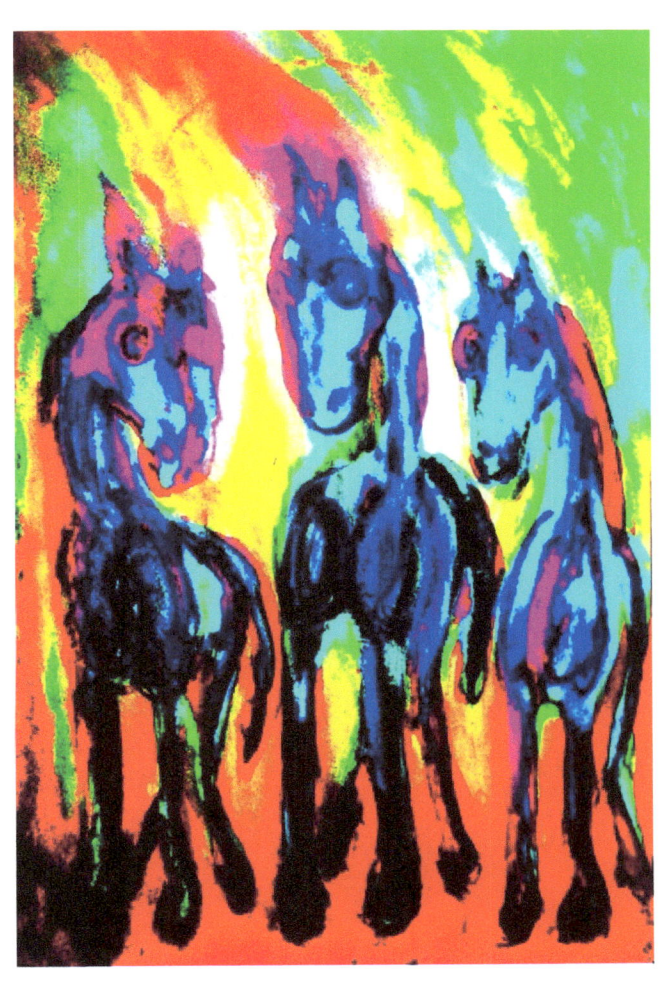

Mother and father and I
in the background.
I was born of a horse,
but I was not a horse.

My sister was my horse
And I was her head and will.
It has been almost an obsession.

I have always painted horses.
It has been almost an obsession.

Where did my horse go?
Why did she leave me?

It is hectic. You are excited, walking energetically around in your studio.

We put our footprints on the semi-wet canvases stretched on the floor.

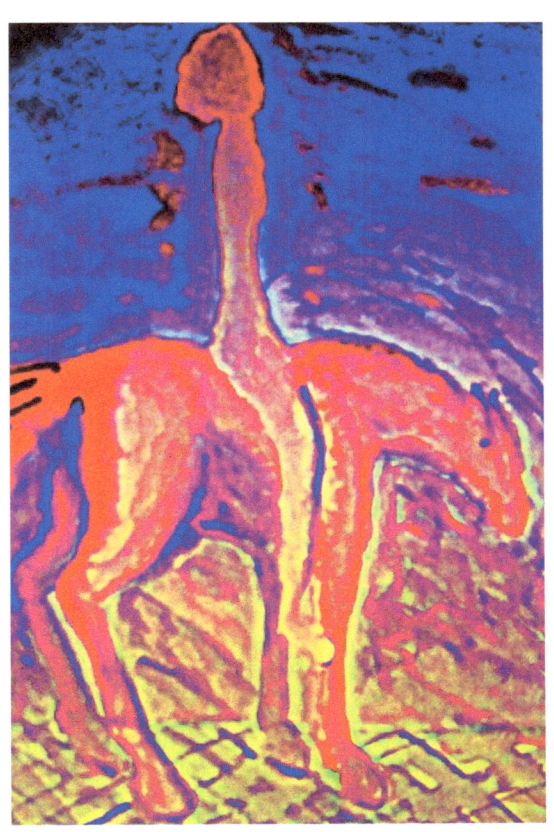

You are characterized
by a clenched energy.
One feels
almost physically
that you feel
it is time to fight
back against critics
who claim that
you are too superficial.

You feel sore.
But you know
The images will
be made.

I have always painted

horses.

It has been almost

an obsession.

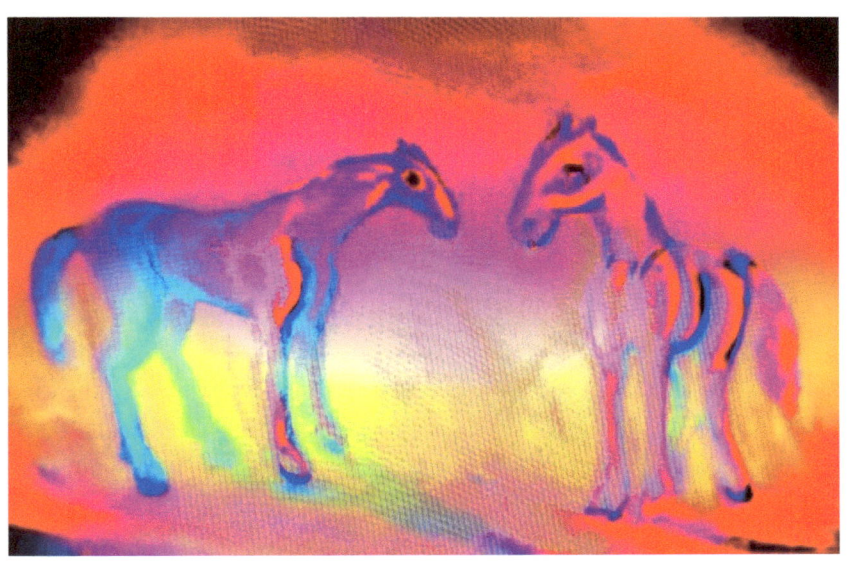

The soul's a horse.

The horse's soul.

The feminine.

The sensuous.

A picture of three horses. Mother,
father and I in the background.
I was born of a horse,
but I was not a horse.
My sister was my horse.

I was her head and will.
It has been almost
an obsession.
I have always painted
horses.
It has been almost
an obsession.
Where did my horse go.
Why did she leave me.

I have read the book

of Job,

Ecclesiastes,

Old Testament.

Many people did.

All old people have

read the Bible.

It is heavy and

powerful.

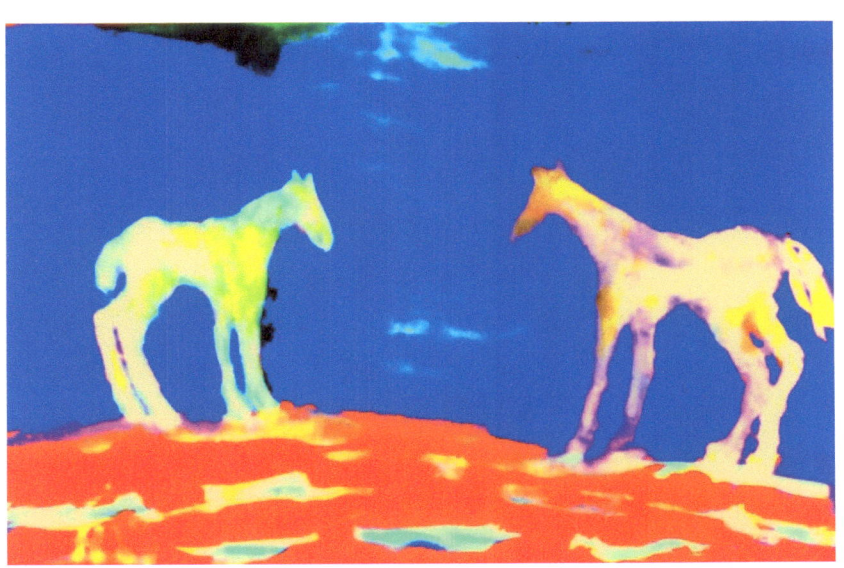

But I tend to carry
my church with me.
I have thought a lot
for myself,
in religious ways too.

I've never been good
at stopping by something.
I'm not good at listening,
And I'm not good
at discussing and
I do not understand
other people's views.

I am in love with my painting,

it is a form for sensuality.

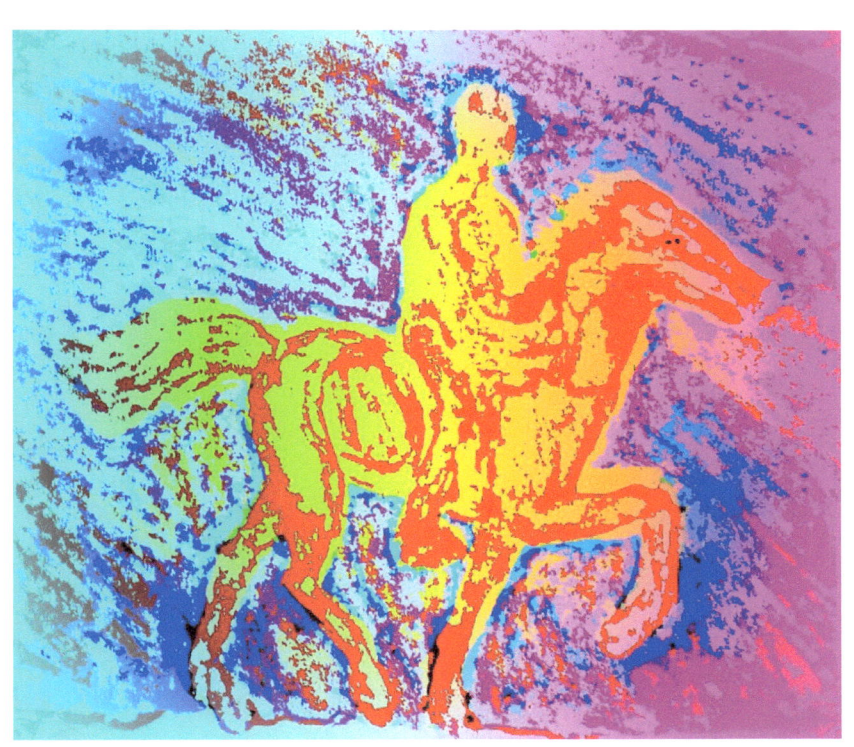

But I know several people

who are just as self-absorbed

as me.

Some people are keen

on control,

to be in control,

knowing

what's going on.

Others are able

to devote themselves

to the extent

that they lose

control.

I drop out

and hope

that it is soil

where I land.

I've forgotten everything

I said last time and

I cannot remember

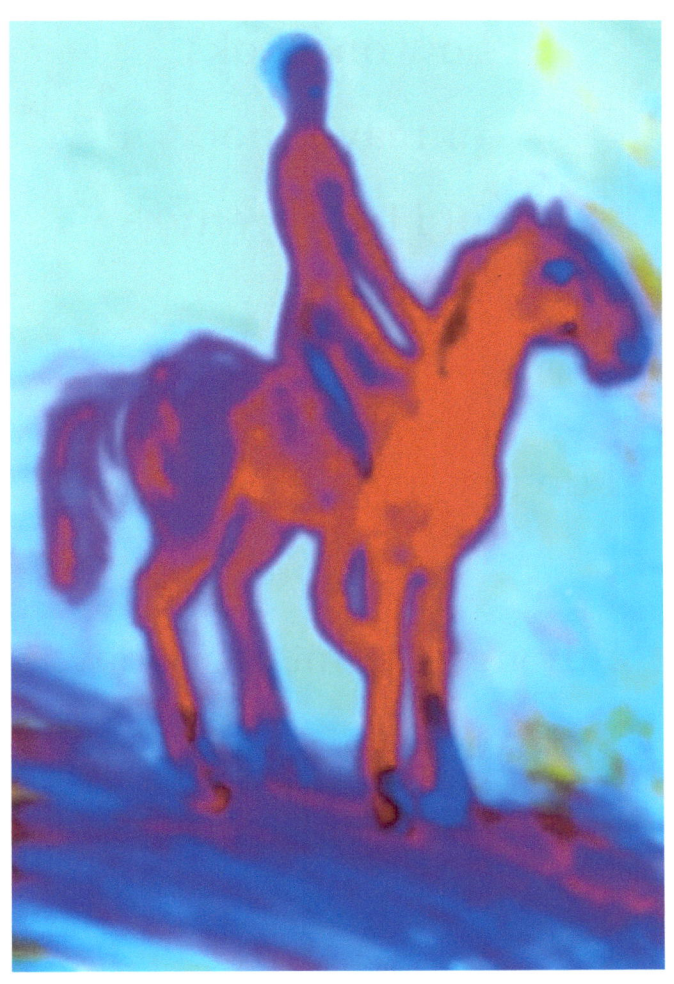

How I looked
On the pictures

It's important
how one looks
or maybe not,
but I look pretty
good now.

I do not enjoy life as much
as before,
although I paint every day.
And I forget a lot.
But this is also good,
in a way.

I don't have to fill my head

with so much.

And I'm not talking

as much as before.

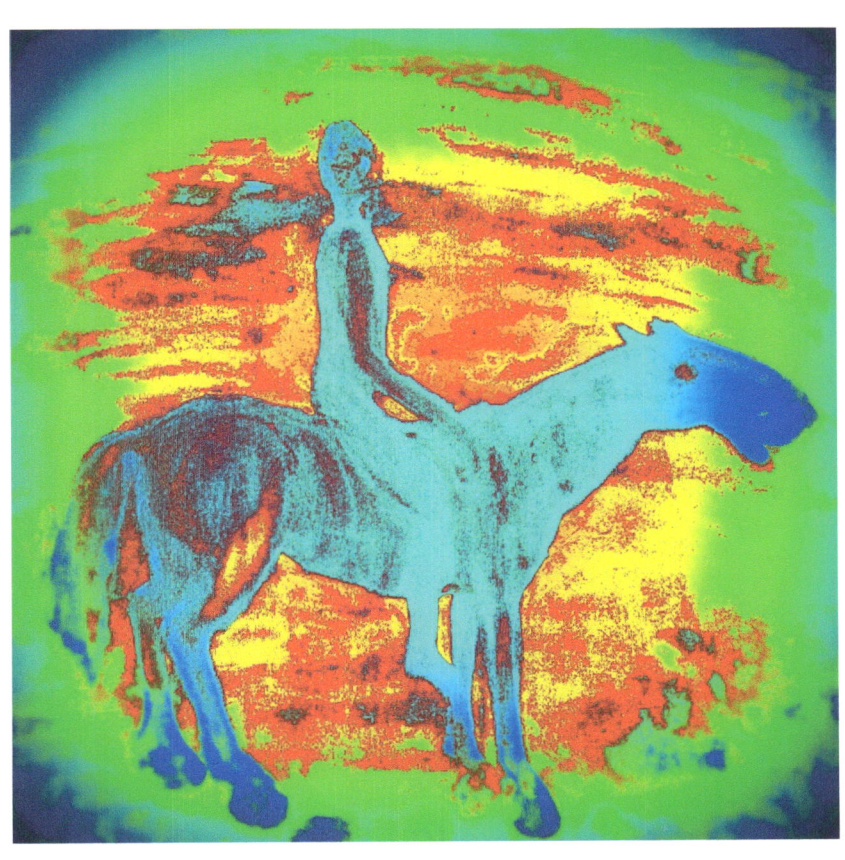

You smile,

A quiet little smile,

looking me deep

into my eyes

with a strong look.

It is not color,

but the light,

I paint.

Look here.

See how the light

illuminates the color

of the flower.

The light creates

the color.

The horse is in me and in you too,

There is a meeting between me,

the horse

and the painting.

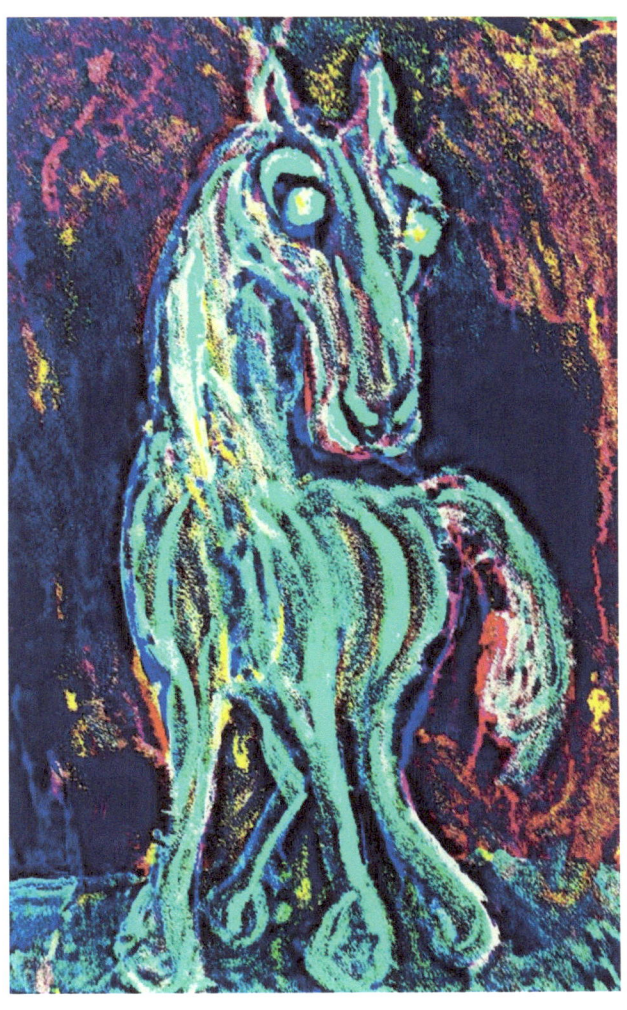

If you are painting

a horse,

you don't know

in advance

how it will be.

You have to let go

and let the feelings go.

The more insecure,

And clumsy you are

and the less control you have,

the better is the horse.

I paint my horses

because it's something

I cannot do.

There are swiftly memories

of the brushstrokes,

energetic and vibrant.

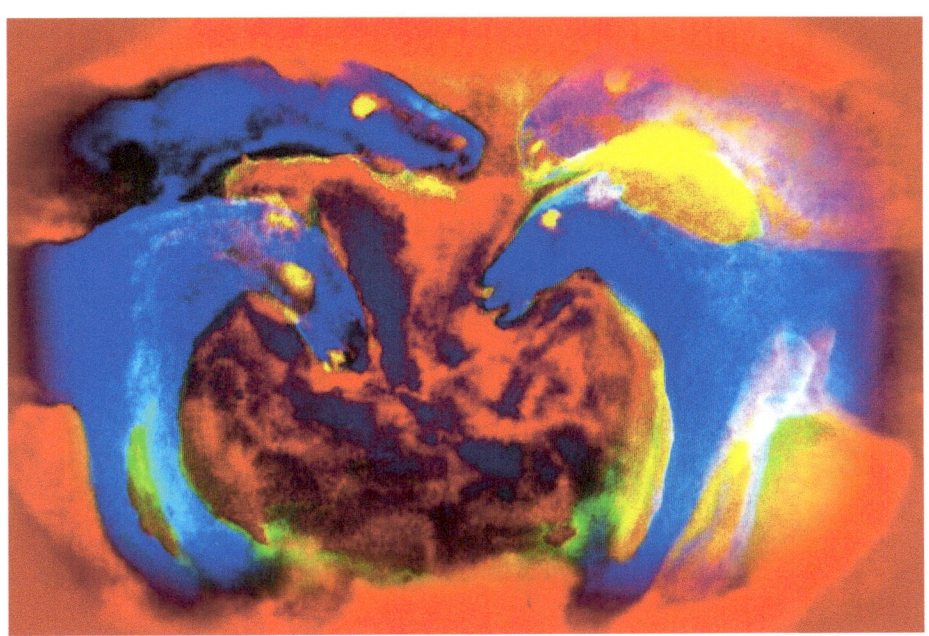

Black and white horses

can also be colorful,

just look at the light

in the woodcut.

I have always painted horses.

It has been almost an obsession.

Mother and father and me

in the background.

I was born of a horse, but

I was not a horse.

My sister was my horse

And I was her

head and will.

It has been almost

an obsession.

I have always painted horses.

It has been almost an obsession.

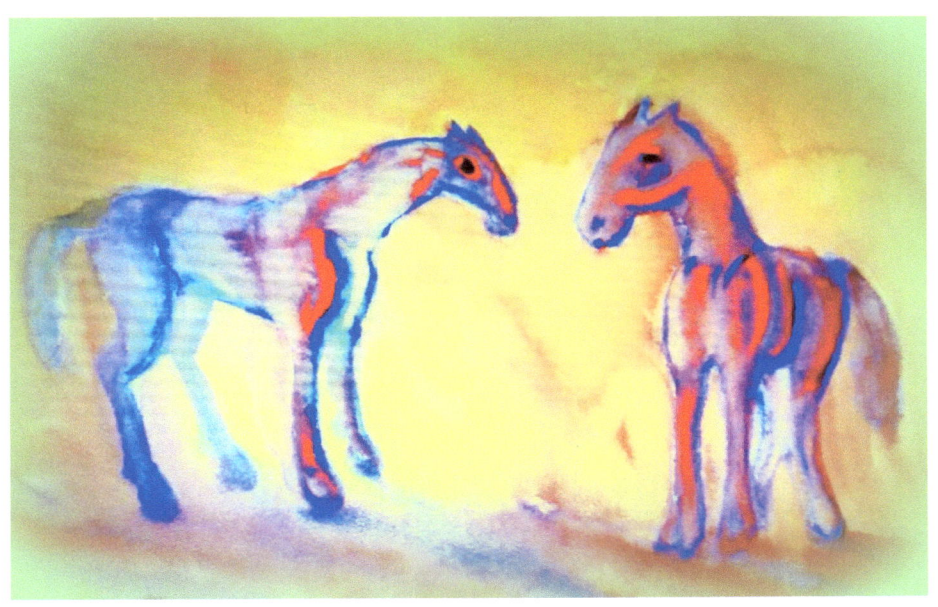

Where

did my horse go?

Why

did she leave me?

My subjects came to me

As from a different dimension,

a spiritual sphere,

but now it strikes me

that it is life

here and now,

I am painting

in real colors.

riders are just ordinary

people who ride around.

There is nothing

heroic about it.

I do not live with a lot of people

as before,

and I cannot get the same contact

with people

and I do not understand

in the same way.

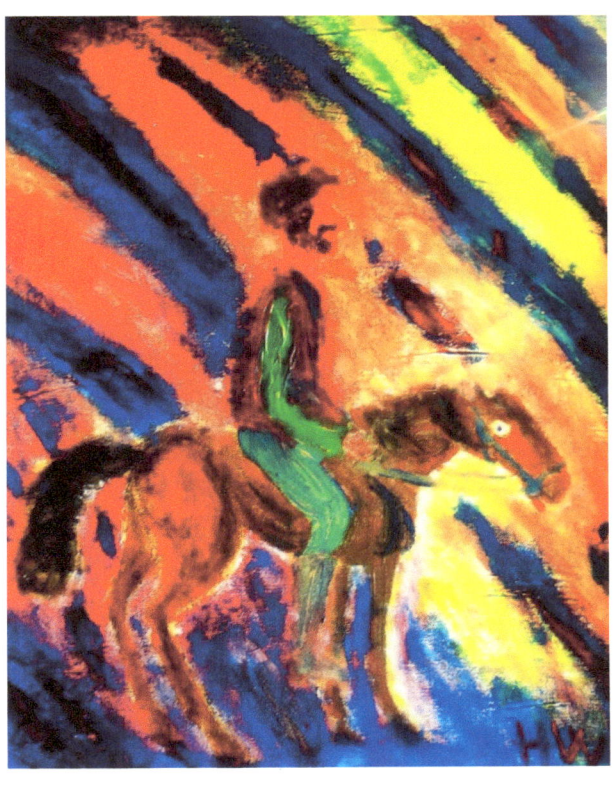

Instead,

I live closer

to the pictures,

and I think even more

than I paint.

What is the problem

In repeating oneself

You connect

To an understanding

of art as an expression

of the innermost

feelings.

Light is the key Element in the pictures, and Light plays

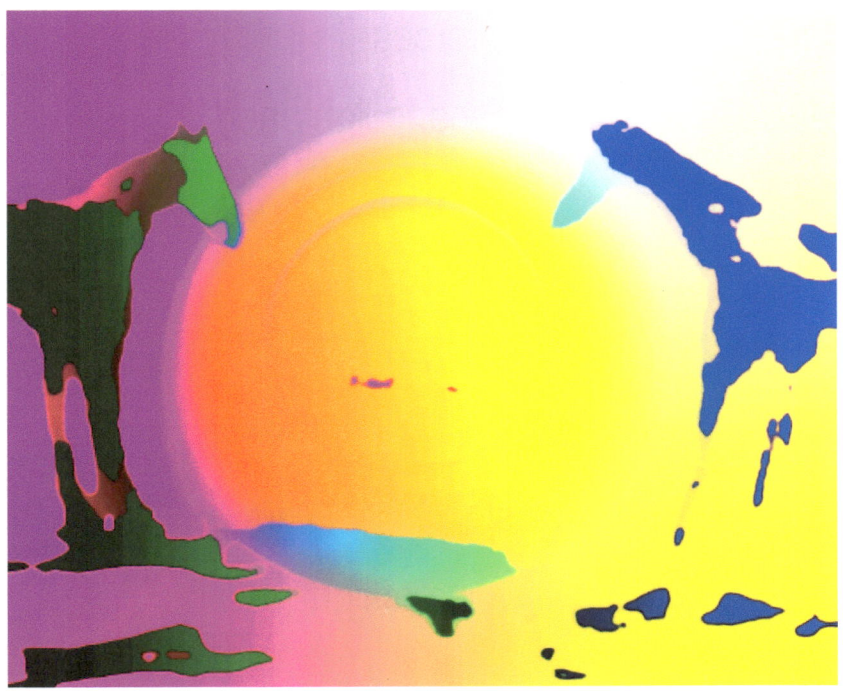

not only the role of significant funding, it is also light the images thematically circle around.

the light represent

vitality

and natural growth

forces

in a landscape lightened

of sunshine.

the love glows

between two people,

or it is spiritual growth,

or existential longing.

the use of light

in the image

makes us ascribe a religious theme.

The continuous circling

of the light.

Not only soul light, but also sunlight,

or the one reflected in the other.

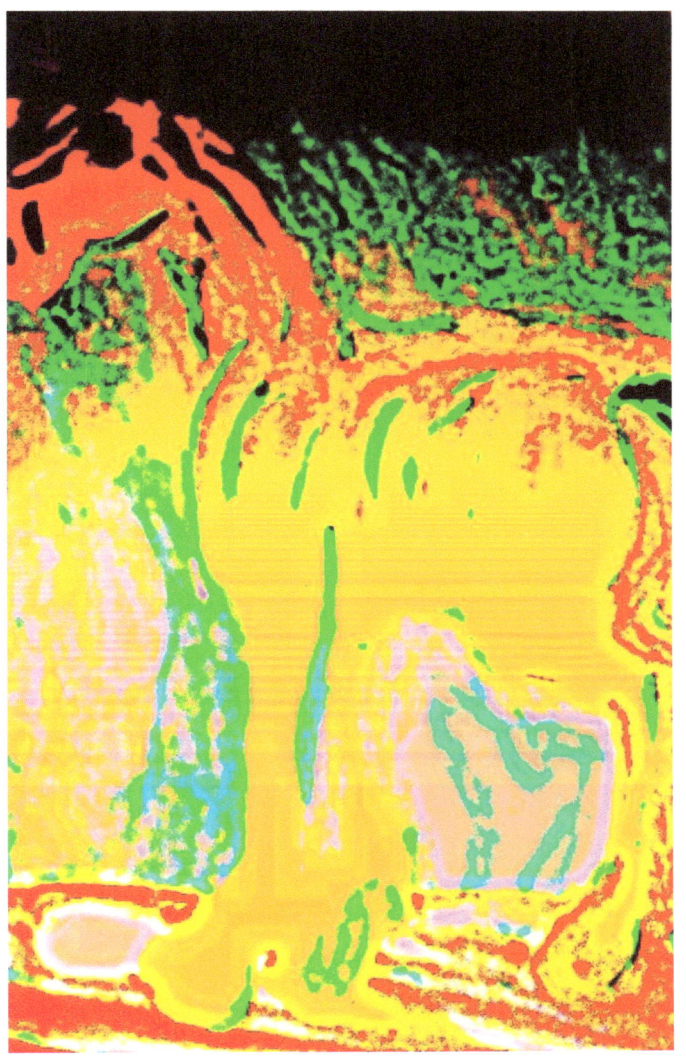

the elongated figures

make it tempting

to imagine the human figure

the rising sun,

where the outline disappears

into the surrounding refractive figure.

You circuit about

Your existential issues.

This fascination with light

ability to prey on the matter we see

in extended use of the human

figure in silhouette,

seems to have been contributing

for living creatures

distinctive appearance.

You have to let go

and let the feelings go.

The more insecure,

And clumsy you are

and less control you have,

the better

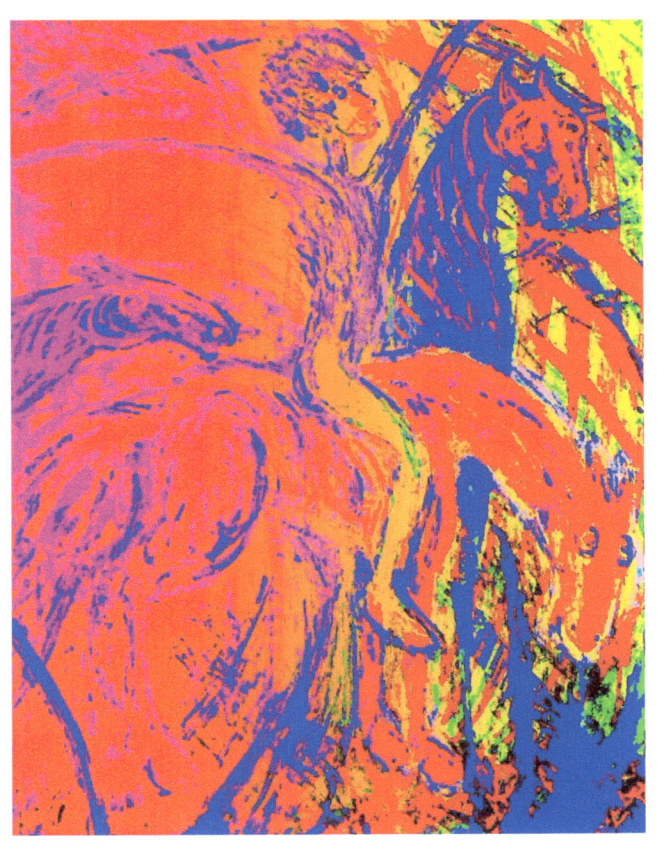

There are some

who are keen

to control,

to be in control,

knowing

what's going on.

Then

there is the other

character type,

which is able

to devote themselves

to the extent

that one loses control.

I'm not good to listen, And I'm not
good At discussing and
I do not understand
other people's views.

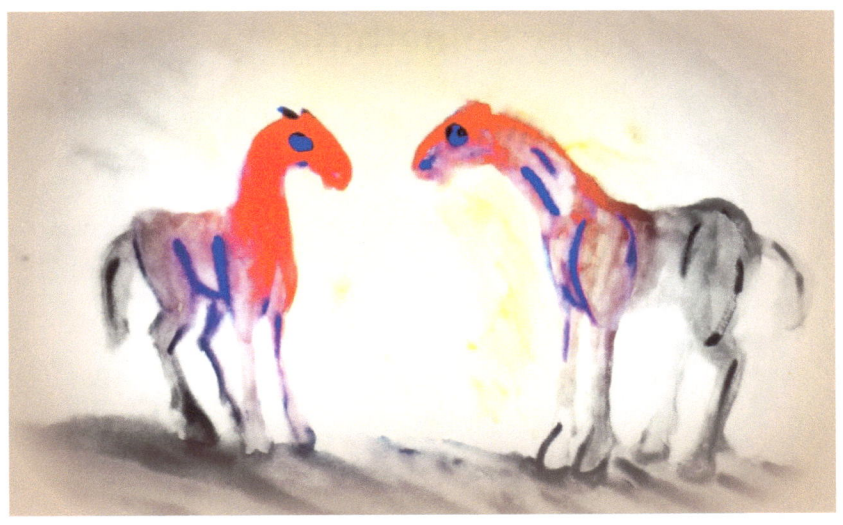

You have to let go and let the feelings
go. The more insecure, And clumsy
you are, and less control you have, the
better

I have thought

A lot for myself,

But I've never

been any good

to stop

by something.

I'm not good to listen,

And I'm not good

At discussing and

I do not understand

other people's views.

I have always painted

horses.

It has been almost

an obsession.

Mother

and father and I

in the background.

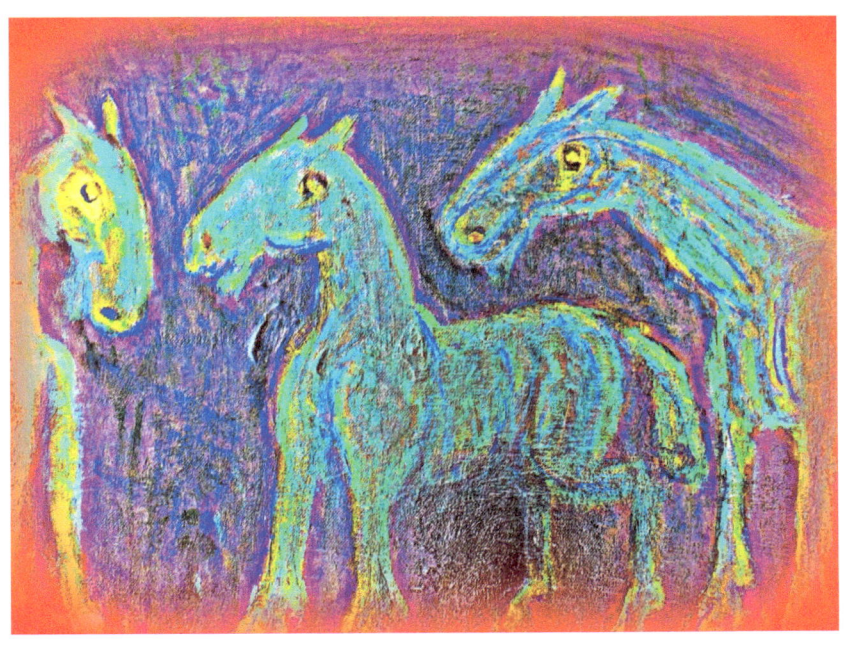

I was born of a horse, but I was not a

horse.

My sister was

my horse

And I was her

head and will.

It has been almost

an obsession.

I have always painted

horses.

It has been almost

an obsession.

Where

did my horse go.

Why

did she leave me.

You circuit about

Your existential issues.

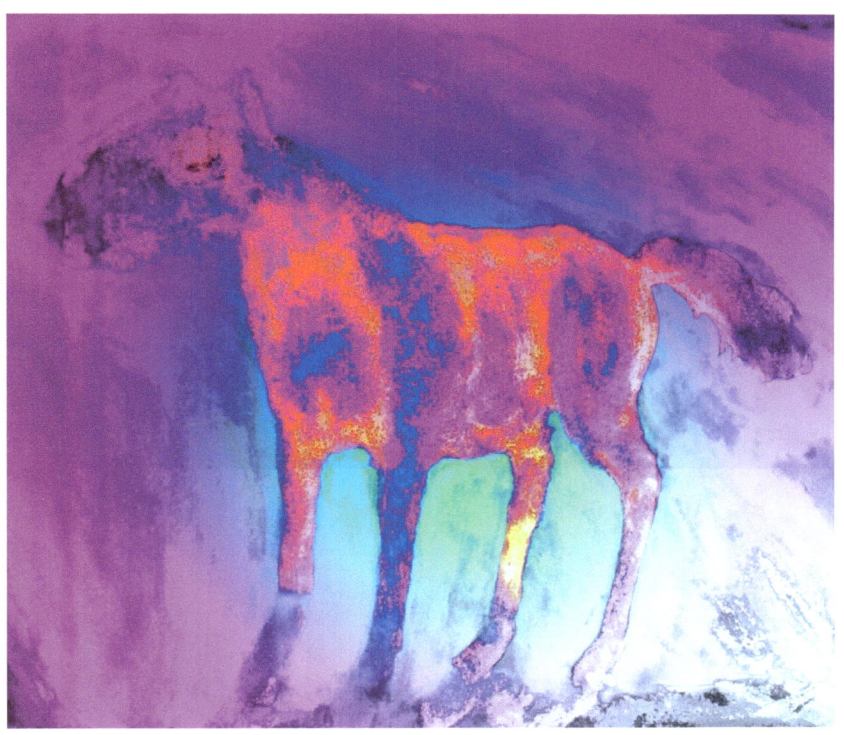

The separate images

are generally worn

by a simplified

existential rhetoric.

say that your pictures

show people in the tension

between freedom

and security,

with classic freedom

metaphors.

So you circuit

about your existential

issues.

You keep the viewer

at a distance.

You walk, float or

spiral out of reach,

alone

or in your heroic solitude.

You also deal

with anxiety,

but not painted

into the pictures

as a theme.

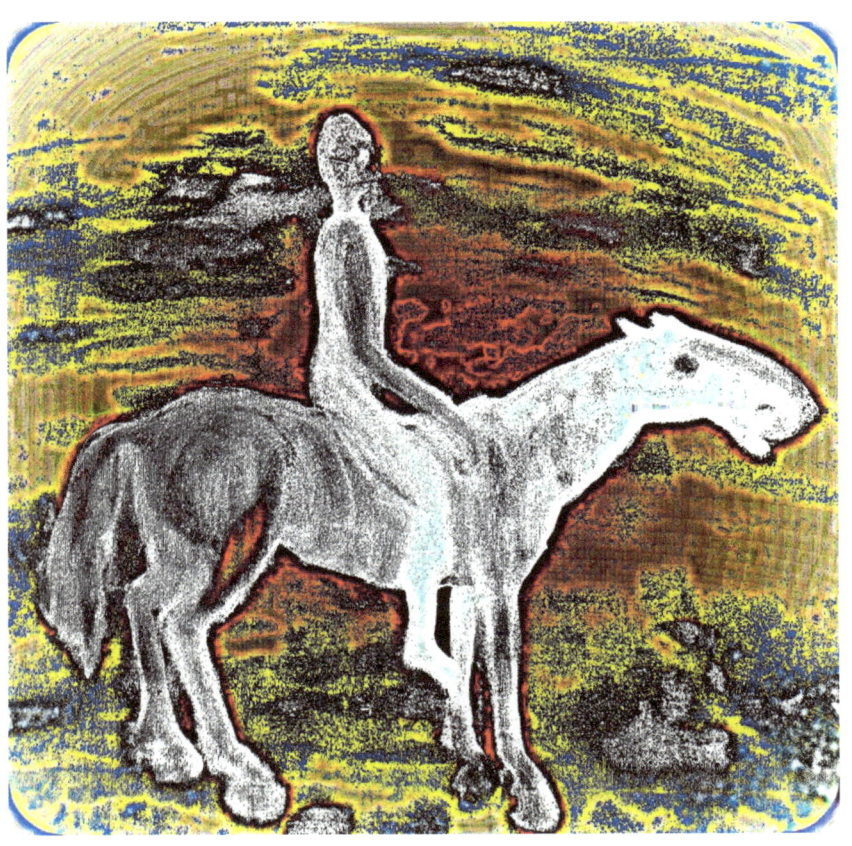

Anxiety occurs

because you abolish

the fundamental nature

of regularities

in the images.

the screaming figure

is elusive and intangible.

In a similar way

You challenge

laws of nature

as you dissolve gravity

People meet,

They form community

and even love.

But despite this

Life is about loneliness.

I have always painted
horses.
It has been almost
an obsession.

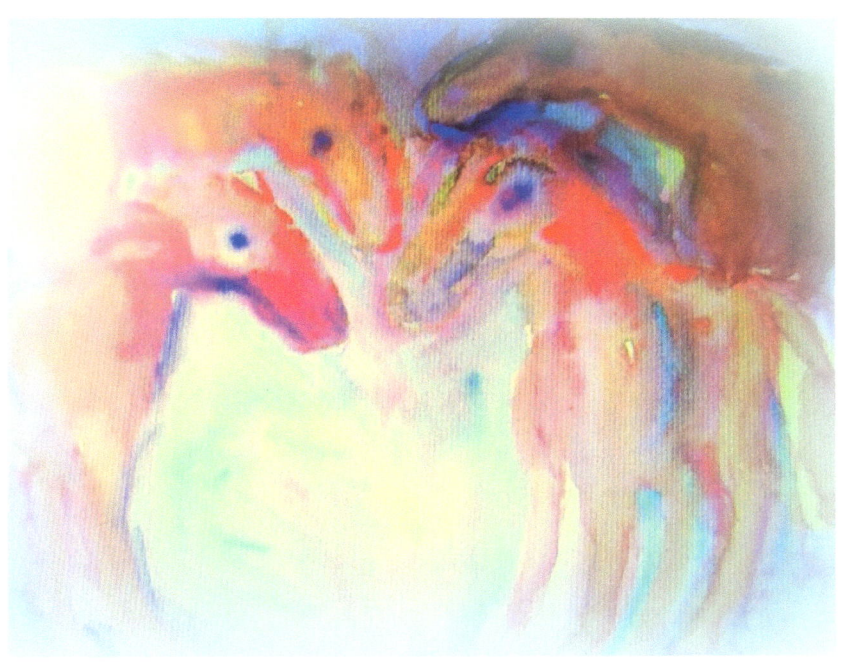

Mother and father and I
in the background.
I was born of a horse, but
I was not a horse.

My sister was my horse

And I was her head and will.

It has been almost an obsession.

I have always painted horses.

It has been almost an obsession.

Nobody understands this.

Where did my horse go?

Why did she leave me?

You walk,

float or

spiral out of reach,

alone

or in your heroic

solitude.

Life is about

Loneliness

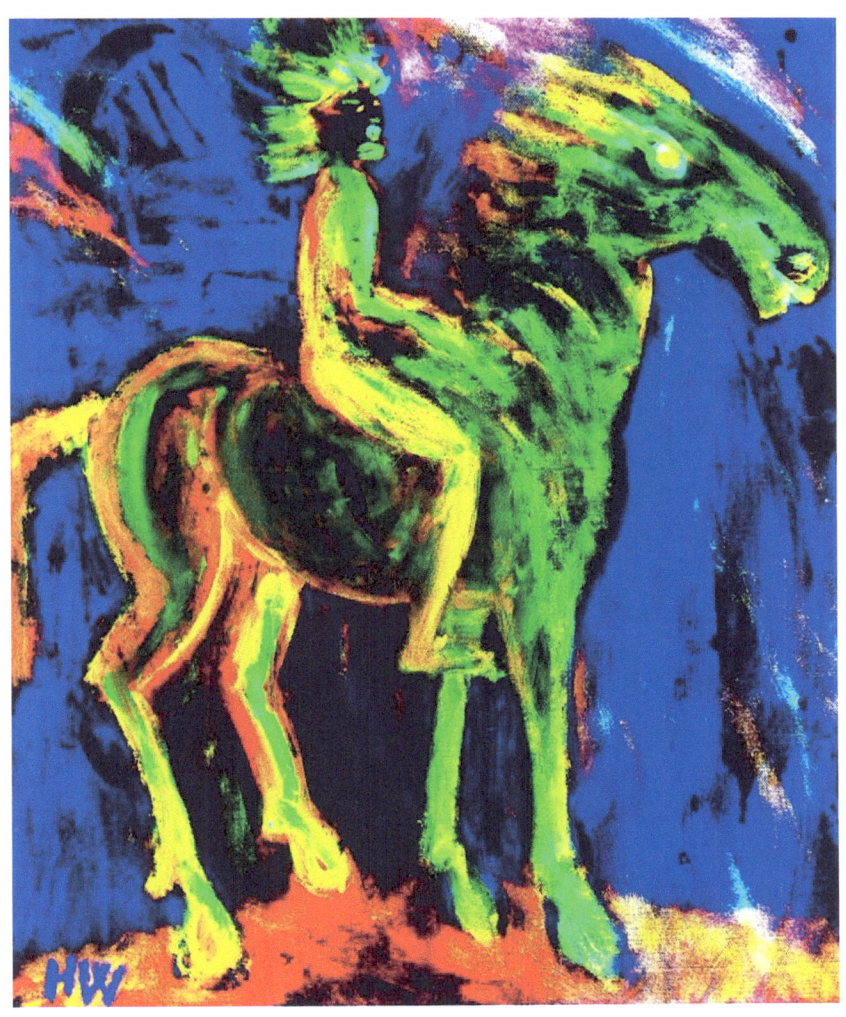

This is not

about individuals

but about a timeless

human existence.

The characters we are confronted with

must be understood as allegories

of human qualities or concepts.

They are presented without a face

or identity, and they are not individuals with

personal characteristics, they are more

general human

As representatives of man

They shall be born and live

in solitude and cohesion,

as love in pain and joy,

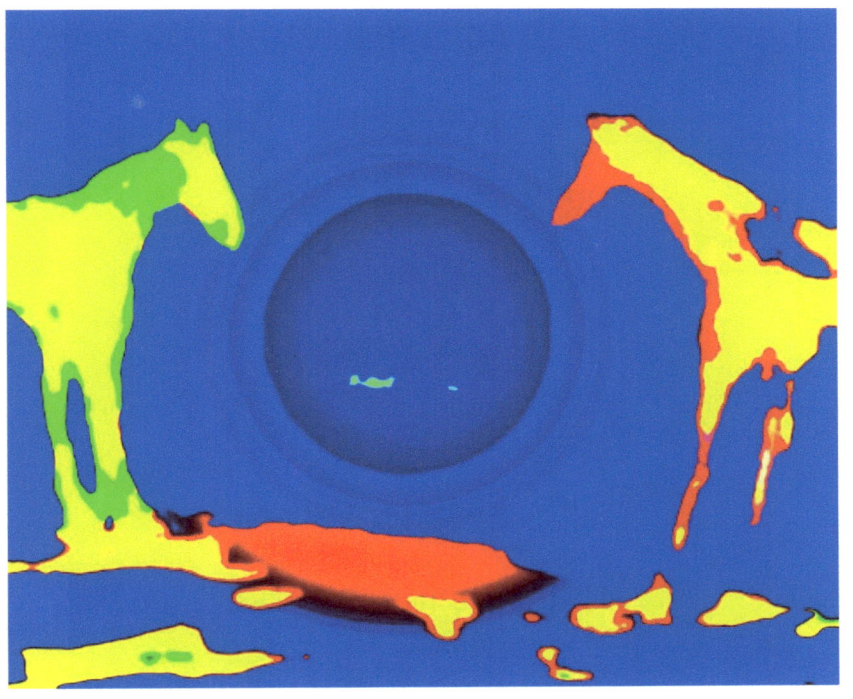

they are not individuals

with personal characteristics,

they are more general human

This is not about individuals,

but about a timeless

human existence.

It is not a real war

we are confronted with,

but war as an eternal

dark quality

of human life.

But do we care?

It is not a real war

we are confronted with,

but war as an eternal

dark quality

of human life.

It is not a real war

You confront us with,

but war as an eternal

dark quality of human life.

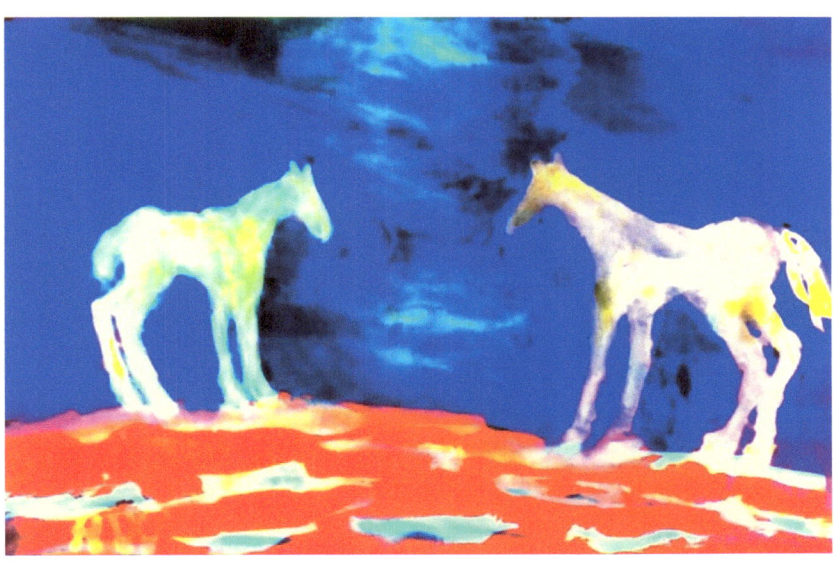

The allusion of something

universal and timeless

makes your images

in danger of being empty clichés.

For what do we care

About Birth, Death or Love in general?

It is not a real war You confront us with, but war

as an eternal

dark quality of human life.

But what do you care

I have always painted

horses.

It has been almost

an obsession. Mother

and father and I in the background.

I was born of a horse, but

I was not a horse.

My sister was

my horse

And I was her

head and will.

It has been almost

an obsession.

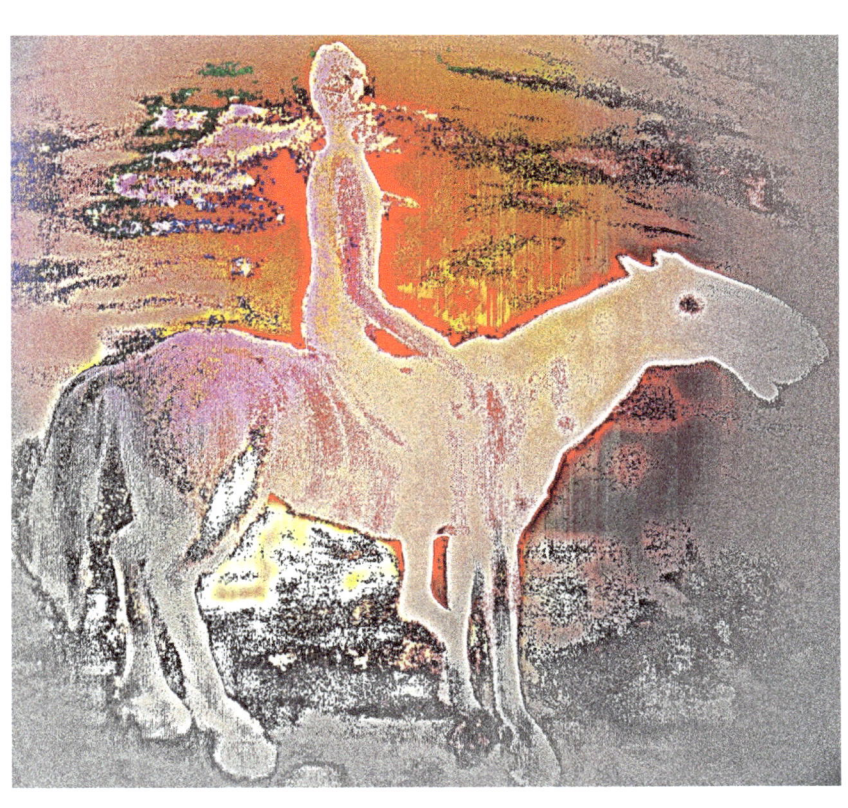

I have always painted horses.

It has been almost

an obsession.

Where did my horse go?

Why did she leave me?

The images express a fervent ambition

to convey eternal truths about reality.

Your artistic project is a quest

for knowledge,

The brain knows and the eye look.

You want to know what you see,

and see what you know.

This is not an exploration

of the painterly medium as such

or concept of art changing status,

but the way the visual and the rational

and knowledge of life itself.

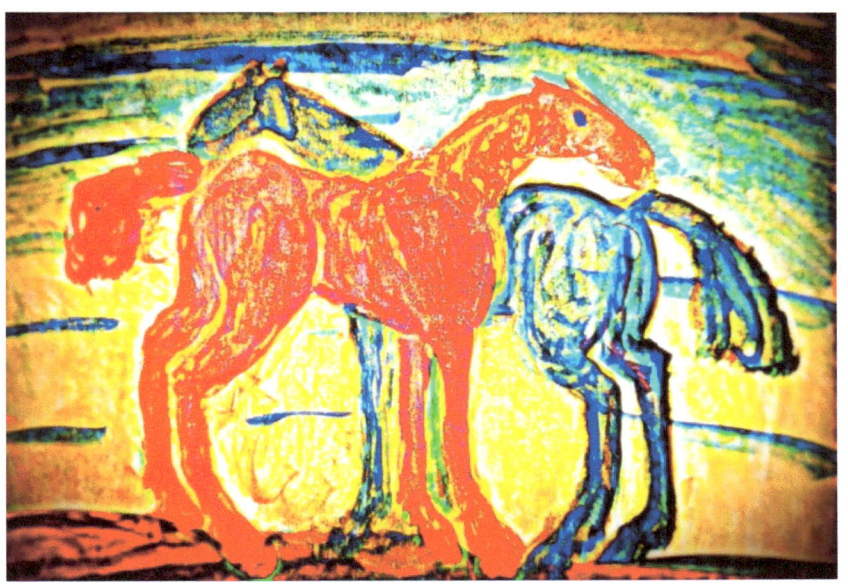

You maintain

your pictures

as a medium

with a privileged access to reality.

You convey a genuine belief in the painting and

its ability

to convey something

of an inner and an outer reality.

You do not see the painting

as one discourse among many.

You see it as the way

to reach understanding.

I have always painted horses.

It has been almost an obsession.

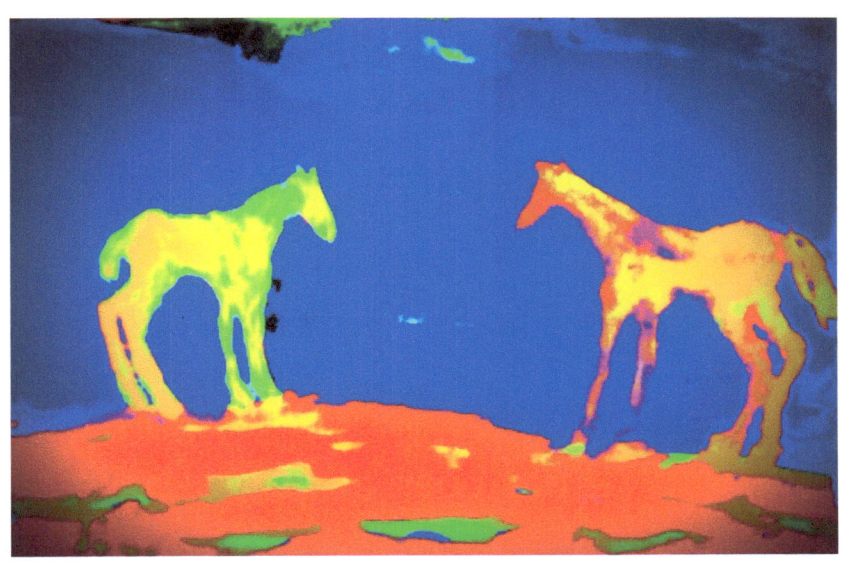

Mother and father and I

in the background.

I was born of a horse, but

I was not a horse.

My sister was

my horse

And I was her head and will.

It has been almost

an obsession.

I have always painted

horses.

It has been almost

an obsession.

Where

did my horse go?

Why

did she leave me?

One may wonder if a prerequisite

for a painting is to be relevant today,

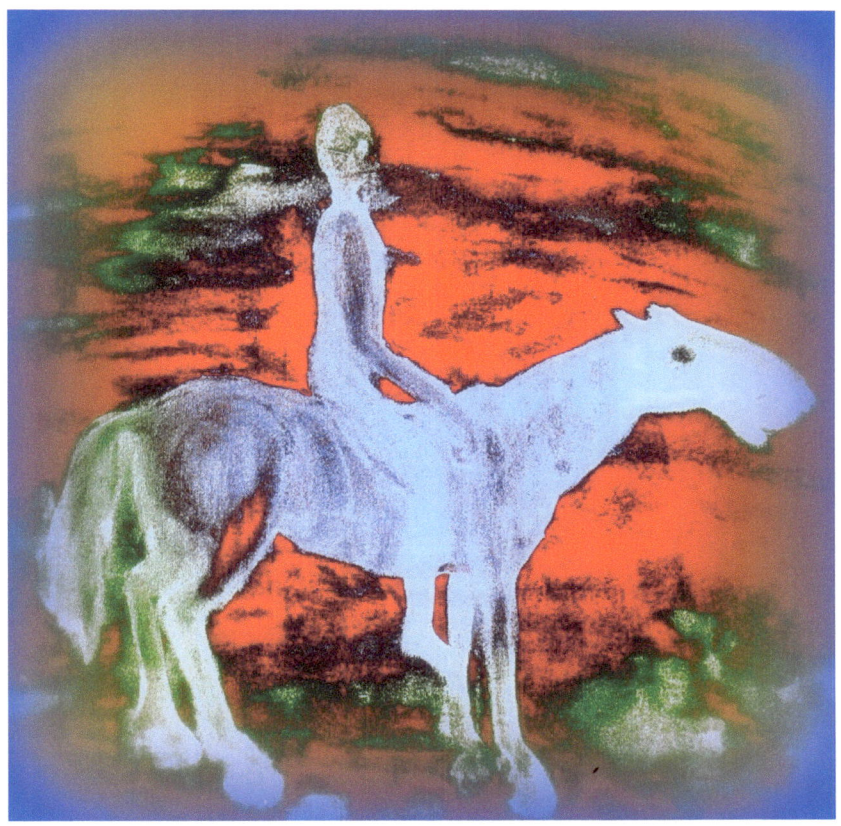

and to some degree involve a critical

awareness of the historical situation.

But this consciousness is entirely absent in

your project.

You have to let go

and let the feelings go.

The more insecure,

And clumsy you are

and less control you have,

the better is the horse.

You borrow freely shapes and forms from a

broad historical tradition.

You let yourself inspire. You are an

impressionist, expressionist

or a symbolic surrealist,

these style designations are more than

a hundred years old.

You are a national icon,

an unstoppable artist

more loved

than controversial.

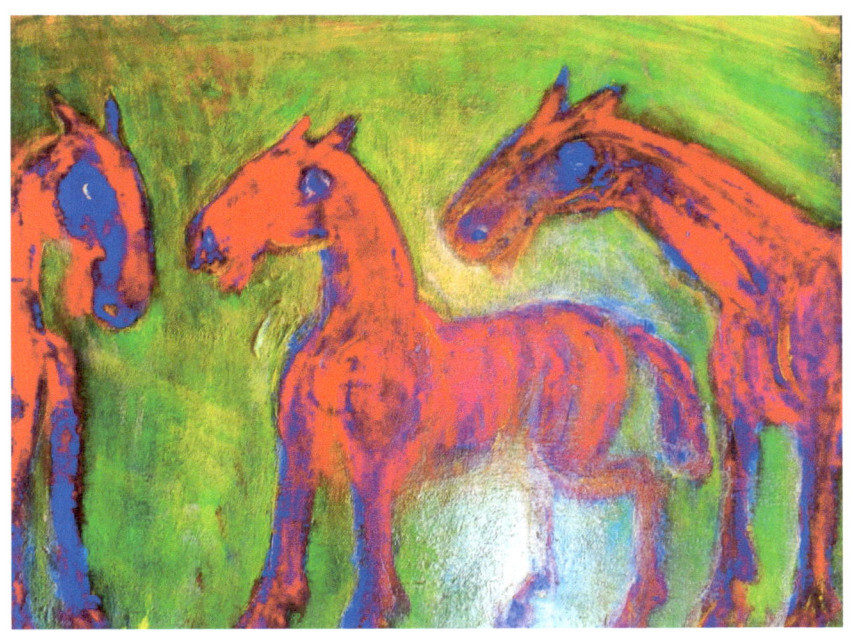

Yet we grown tired of you,

Your pictures are exhausted,

we saw it all twenty years ago.

But you don't give up.

What is it with you? Why can't you stop? Have you forgotten that you have done it all before?

I have always painted horses.
It has been almost an obsession.
Mother and father and I
in the background.
I was born of a horse, but
I was not a horse.
My sister was a horse
And I was her head and will.
It has been almost
an obsession.

I have always painted horses.

It has been almost

an obsession.

Where did my horse go?

Why did she leave me?

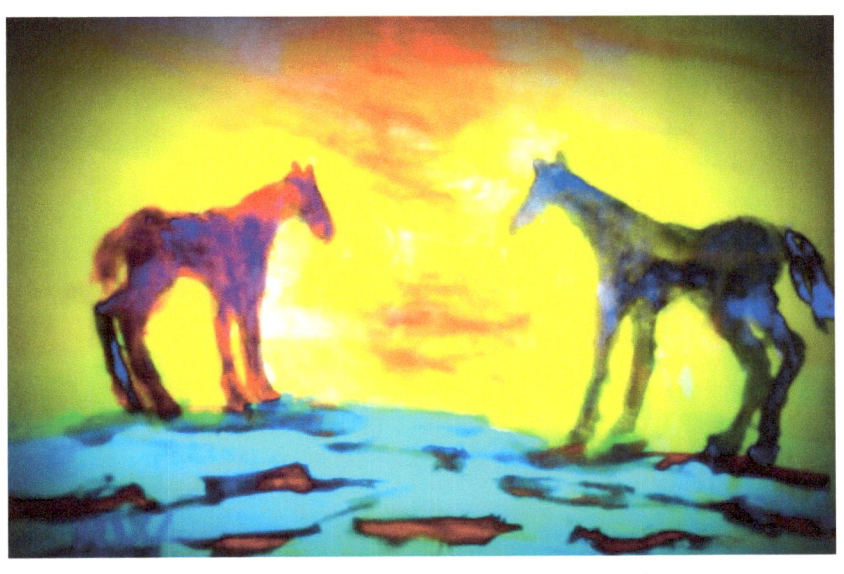

She is dead now and nobody

understands me anymore.

www.ingramcontent.com/pod-product-compliance
Lightning Source LLC
Chambersburg PA
CBHW040810200526
45159CB00022B/134